Copyright

Get This As a FREE Audiobook via Amazon's Audible.com

Visit: Bookskim.com/free

How to Build a Strong CRM Database for Marketing

CRM marketing is a powerful tool that many marketers are still overlooking today, yet it can make you more efficient and increase your marketing efforts.

If someone asked you how many customers you had in your region, could you tell them? If you were asked how many sales prospects, you had, would you know?

Using CRM it is important to divide your customer data base into segments or regions, because if you don't when you send out that email message, everyone is going to get it and at best it will result in a low response and worse it will annoy customers and have them drop off your mailing list. So how does one build a strong database that will improve your marketing results?

1. Watch Your Data Quality

At the base of your marketing being effective is the need for access to good quality data. You need to get as much information on a company or person as you can. You can uses

Google or LinkedIn to find out more about a person. There are other business directories that can be helpful. The minimum information you should have is their address, telephone number, email and title. You can also add your interests. Add the information you find to your CRM database.

2. Maintain a Good Database

In order to maintain a good database you need to be updating it regularly. This should not just be the job of the marketing department but it should also involve other departments that access the information. They will also have opportunities to update information. For example, a customer phones in with a complaint and they the customer service rep a new phone number, they need to be adding it at that stage. This is how good solid databases are built.

3. Have the Ability to Select

When you have created structured data, it is easy for you to choose based on your target group. You can select one or more target groups for your marketing campaign to target. For example, maybe you want to run an email campaign that targets those people with the title 'account manager' and who are assigned to the salesperson Joey. You will access your CRM software and select with this criteria. It will take no time at all for the list to appear on the screen. There's no need for Excel or large complicated processes.

If staff understands the importance of filling in as many fields as possible, you will create a powerful database full of customer information and your marketing campaigns will become stronger and more powerful.

Blending Marketing and Your CRM

CRM has long been used by many businesses. After all, it has significant value in the management of customers and the associated data. But the world is changing and so is the way we do business. Today's customer is actually 57 percent into the buying cycle before they even talk to anyone from the company. Now more than ever before, when a customer reaches out, a marketer must be there through all the steps.

When the right CRM software is used it will allow your marketers to plan and execute campaigns across a number of channels from beginning to end, and then it will allow you to measure the effectiveness of those campaigns. CRM can allow you to build your sales pipeline across numerous channels and to demonstrate in real time the impact of your marketing investment.

With the ability to streamline, plan and execute you can create an integrated plan to fit your budget and then track and analyze across all of your channels. You'll be able to reach your prospects through digital methods, email, social networking and more traditional means. You can collaborate processes and manage them across all your marketing team from one platform. Marketing has never been easier.

Because you can now easily design the journey of your customer or prospect, the recipient is receiving highly targeted content whether it's a newsletter or a special offer. You can now easily create different channels to target different markets. In addition, you can make your emails interactive so that you can record valuable information based on the actions of the recipient. This additional information helps you to even fine tune your target markets even further.

You can seamlessly build your sales pipeline and follow your prospects through that pipeline. You can boost the interest of prospects through multistage marketing campaigns that deliver personalized content. With CRM, you can combine your marketing and sales funnels.

CRM allows you to keep the sales team in the loop. You can easily provide your sales team with access to the marketing calendar so they know exactly what campaigns are running and what to expect coming down the pipe.

One of the most powerful tools you have available is marketing analytics. You can now easily measure ROI and get a real time view of your effectiveness. These clear views of your marketing campaigns mean you can quickly change or fine-tune any campaign based on its performance.

Marketing is essential to the success of your business and CRM should play an important role in today's marketing strategies. Don't get left out in the cold.

How to Improve Your CRM to Benefit Your Marketing

If you want to succeed with your business, you need loyal customers and brand loyalty. Building customer relationships is critical, as is feedback. But you need to be able to balance what they want with giving into requests. This is where your CRM software comes into play. It helps you to build a complete customer profile that includes their feedback. It helps you to build a relationship with your customers. Marketing involves existing customers and new lead generation. Here we'll focus on marketing to those existing customers and how your CRM can benefit you.

1. Word of Mouth – Candid Conversations

In our world today, most people spend at least part of their day on technology whether it's their computer, tablet, or smartphone. When it comes to deciding what to buy or where to buy it word of mouth has always played an important role and it still does today, just in a somewhat different format called social media. This is also the fastest and most effective way to build trust with customers and prospects. It's also known to give the highest ROI. This includes online reviews, recommendations, open questions and answers, feedback and more. These conversations and what you learn about your customers can be integrated into your CRM software.

2. Be Honest

One way that small business stands out over large businesses is that customers have an easier time talking to a real live human. That translates to a lot less of their valuable time used trying to get a response and the building of trust in their relationship with the company. Always be honest with your customer. Even when your customer is in the wrong, you can be respectful and kind in your response. Your CRM software helps you to see patterns that are established, such as customers that tend to complain often or who have phoned in with the same problem or complaint numerous time.

But what does that have to do with marketing. Well, as you create marketing campaigns that target through social media, you will be asked questions about your product, and it is important that you answer these prospects in an honest manner as well. In addition, you need to be incorporating these questions and responses into your CRM database so that you can follow them through the pipeline and determine how long it is from the initial engagement until the second sale takes place. In some cases, this can be quite long.

3. Keep Track of Your Customers and Prospects

Every conversation with a customer needs to be recorded and their CRM customer profile upgraded. All of this information is key to creating marketing campaigns that correctly target the desired audience. When a customer first purchases the initial information is recorded in the CRM database, but that profile needs to be continuously added to and built upon for marketing to be the most effective it can be.

How to Take Advantage of CRM Marketing Strategies

In a world that revolves around software technology, marketing has quickly evolved in just a matter of a few years. Thanks to the internet, marketing has never been more accessible and more affordable than it is right now. It allows marketers to target a specific market with a specific marketing campaign far more frequently and with a much broader reach.

However, ironically, the digital age flexibility has actually made some marketers more ineffective because potential customers become irritated by messages that are not relevant or that arrive too often, customers become confused with messages that conflict, and a failure to connect to an audience that has had too much exposure.

CRM has added a new strength to the online marketing world because marketers have those challenges addressed. CRM is far more than just software that manages your customers contact information and call notes. Previous versions of CRM software were able to help sales people and marketers focus marketing activities because it allowed for data mining. Today's CRM software is proactive. Rather than trying to understand the data that's been entered, today's CRM is able to create, correlate, and display information visually to help you identify sales opportunities and patterns.

CRM can help you identify your target audience and the product, create your target list, decide what your message will be and then distribute it, via the medium you decide to use. You could opt for delivery via website, mail out, email, phone, etc. You can automate the scheduling. Then you can capture inquiries and replies from your marketing campaign, route them to the correct department or sales staff and track the sales progress in the pipeline. The sale is then recorded and the ROI on the campaign can be determined. You determine your budget and make an ROI forecast for your campaign.

CRM can even help you to determine when the best time is to contact your customer, what kinds of messages get the best response, what new products/services your R&D should be focusing on and even whether your customer is serious about buying or just shopping and comparing.

CRM can do all of this because it can easily be integrated with external mail services, etc. that allow you to create lists that target a specific audience and then import it into your software or in many cases the CRM has these features built in so you can create campaigns and they emails have code embedded into them that ensures the interaction that occurs between you and the person receiving the message to be captured in your CRM database. There's no longer a need to cut and paste.

Today's CRM is not a passive tool. It can give you a full 360-degree look at your customer. These systems can be strategic and tactical with powerful support to make decisions. Capitalize what your CRM software has to offer.

Know the Benefits of Using CRM for Marketing

CRM can really help you with your marketing, which is pretty exciting for marketers. Let's look at just how a CRM system can help you to be more effective with your marketing and turn up the sales.

1. Access to Lead Information is Readily Available

When a CRM system is working right, the sales and marketing are completely integrated. This makes the lead intelligence immediately accessible to the marketers. All of the data is easily accessible and it's all in one place. So whatever marketing software you are using, because it's integrated, your sales team just adds the information in your CRM system, and they will have access to all of your information as well. However, marketers will have better lead information through CRM, because much of the lead intel is gathered in the CRM system not the marketing software. Information can be constantly added as sales team members learn things about the customer. This will mean anyone dealing with that customer will have the 'whole picture' and that makes it easier to target marketing campaigns far more effectively.

2. It Helps With Pipeline Prioritizing

CRM gives you full visibility of the sales pipeline and it also assists you in prioritizing who you are going to email or call first. You never have to miss an opportunity. When both the sales and marketing departments have access they can identify the fields that will be important to them and use a lead scoring system or sifting system – either will work. It give both marketers and sales staff power to make the most out of the best opportunities and to search the pipeline for leads that are at a specific stage in the buying cycle.

3. Sale and Marketing Align Better

CRM won't solve your sales and marketing alignment problems but it does make it better. Each month both departments have numbers they need to meet and if both teams are working in the CRM system that is integrated with your marketing software, it becomes quick and easy to assess the progress of both teams as well as identify and problem areas.

Reports can be generated for management in no time at all. In addition, if marketing is meeting their monthly goals, they can assess whether these leads are filling the pipeline.

That's just 3 ways that you can benefit from using CRM software in your marketing campaigns. Creating a flow that is easy to access, follow and use is key to any successful campaign.

5 Tips to Increase Your Social CRM Success

Social CRM can play an important role in your marketing strategies, especially in a world that is hyperactive around social networking. Let's look at 5 things you can do to increase your social CRM success.

1. Ensure Your Social Media Messages Are in Alignment With Your Brand Image

Even with social media, visitors want to feel like it's a real live person they are talking with. You want to ensure the tone of your messages on your social media sites are in alignment with your company. For example, a laid back coffee house that caters to university students can have a casual, relaxed tone on their social media page, but a big corporation dealing with money investment must be professional, courteous and information. In other words, know what your brand image is and who your audience is.

2. A Timely Responses to Customers is Necessary

How fast you respond to a customer is as important as your response. The faster the better. We live in a world of 'instant' and so when a customer asks a question they want an answer immediately. They should not have to wait hours for their answer. This is especially true if they have a complaint. You will have to work at staying on top of it, but the reward it customer trust and loyalty.

3. Take Advantage of the Group Feature

Thankfully, the three most important social networks (LinkedIn, Facebook and Twitter) make this simple. You can easily create groups such as Prospects, Current Customers, Positive Feedback, etc. You can then create social campaigns for each group of visitors. This is a very helpful tool.

4. Be as Human as Possible – Put a Name & a Face to It

People on social media want to interact with 'real people' not with nameless corporate entities. When you are building relationships on your social networking make sure that you are using your name and it's a good idea to have a picture of yourself attached to your ID.

5. Use Your CRM System to Track More on Your Customer

Integrating your social networking with your CRM system allows you to record far more information on your customer. Don't let an opportunity pass you by. This is a great way to build your customer profile, which in turn will help you to be able to create marketing campaigns that are even more targeted.

Social networks are an important part of today's marketing strategies; make sure you get the most out of your social CRM.

Benefits of CRM in Your Marketing

When you combine CRM with marketing automation, you get more than a new system. You create a powerful marketing and sales tool that can improve the quality of your lead generation, make your market to sales handoff more efficient, automate marketing campaigns, and do much more. Marketers will enjoy better marketing accountability and find it easier to see ROI. Let's look at 3 benefits to blending CRM and marketing software.

1. You Can Automate Lead Qualification

One of the biggest problems between sales and marketing teams is that the quality of the leads is poor. Gathering data using a marketing automation system allows marketers to score and grade their leads. That means the highest qualified leads go directly to sales. Leads that reach a specific score threshold and grade are automatically assigned to sales personal. This really cuts down the amount of manual processing that has to happen. The lead assignments are more effective and efficient.

2. Improve the Quality of Revenue Tracking

When your CRM and marketing automation system are integrated, ROI reporting on campaigns is far easier. Bi directional syncing means that campaigns you create in your marketing automation platform map directly back to your CRM software. This allows closed deals to be tied back to the campaign they occurred in. Closed leap reporting increases the quality of the reporting and allows for accurately measuring ROI and projected revenue, tracking marketing spends, and attributing revenue to a specific marketing campaign.

3. Allows for More Targeted Messages to Occur

The majority of buyers want to receive different targeted content at every state of research. In fact, a recent study said 77% want this (Pardot's 2013 State of Demand Generation Study). This behavioral information that marketing automation tool collects can be used to send a targeted message to your prospects. These emails can be very personalized and they can attract the interest of the prospect at the various stages of

When your CRM and marketing automation system are integrated, ROI reporting on campaigns is far easier. Bi directional syncing means that campaigns you create in your marketing automation platform map directly back to your CRM software. This allows closed deals to be tied back to the campaign they occurred in. Closed leap reporting increases the quality of the reporting and allows for accurately measuring ROI and projected revenue, tracking marketing spends, and attributing revenue to a specific marketing campaign.

3. Allows for More Targeted Messages to Occur

The majority of buyers want to receive different targeted content at every state of research. In fact, a recent study said 77% want this (Pardot's 2013 State of Demand Generation Study). This behavioral information that marketing automation tool collects can be used to send a targeted message to your prospects. These emails can be very personalized and they can attract the interest of the prospect at the various stages of the buying cycle. The creation of one on one email communication based on criteria will increase the relevance of your emails and that's going to make costumers happy.

There are many other benefits to incorporating CRM with marketing automation, but these three key points should be enough to get your attention. Much of today's marketing is carried out through email and social media, as well as, a company website. The combination of these two tools can increase the effectiveness of your marketing campaigns.

How to Achieve Success with Social CRM

We live in a hyper social world and that's also where you will find your customers sharing their opinions, offering compliments and voicing their complaints about your products/services. Facebook and Twitter are the two most commonly used social networks but there are many others. It is difficult to separate customer relationship management from social media management; however, just having social CRM alone isn't adequate. You will need to choose a management solution that fits your company and then develop guidelines and strategies that work within it.

Let's look at how you can create a successful social CRM strategy.

1. You Need the Right Resources

Social networks allow you an opportunity like never before to deliver your customers great service. However, your team is setup to solve problems it can be a frustrating experience for your customers. Consumers are extremely impatient with hold times on the phone, but they are also becoming impatient with how social help requests are handled, so keep this in mind.

2. You Need a Solid Platform to Conduct Social CRM

You want to choose a comprehensive social media management platform so that you have quality listening, top-notch engagement capabilities and the ability to monitor. Your social platform needs to seamlessly integrate with your CRM system and it should be customer centered. Off point solutions are a thing of the past.

3. Reward Your Customers That Are Loyal

Those customers that exclusively engage with your brand via social media should be rewarded. You can create a loyalty code to keep those customers. You can also offer a discount code for prospects to entice them to make that purchase. If a customer leaves a positive feedback, reward them by sending them out a personalized message with a discount offer. Send it via snail mail for extra impact.

4. Identify Who Your Social Influencers are and then Engage Them

Use the social media tools available to you to identify who is responsible for driving the most conversation around your brand. Then reach out to those individuals and start to build a relationship with them. Measured Analytics is an excellent tool to use here.

5. Remember to Talk to Your Customers

If you want to build a powerful social media presence, you will need to engage your customers and visitors in two-way conversation don't just shove information out there for them. No one likes to be talked at.

Implement these 5 tips to help you get the most out of your social CRM endeavors.

CRM Experts Share 6 Top Marketing Tips

CRM experts know that your CRM system can play a key role in your marketing campaign. Let's see what the top 6 marketing tips are.

1. Use the Subscription Management Page to Gather Marketing Data

Don't just use the subscription management page to allow recipients to opt out or change their email preferences. Make the most of it. Use it gather additional marketing data. For example, you can use a web form to gather support requests or you can use a survey to obtain your customer's feedback. Make the most out this opportunity to engage with the customer.

2. Do Not Just Use Email Communication for Your Nurture Program

Your nurture campaign should involve both email and a personal phone call from the sales staff. You can trigger a CRM workflow from within the nurture. This will create a reminder for the sales staff to follow up with this customer on the nurtured lead.

3. Use Dynamic Content to Simplify Email Marketing Campaigns

There is no need to create tons of various email templates to send the same message to different audiences that you are targeting. Just create a single template and then take advantage of dynamic content creating a customized experience for the email recipients.

4. Manage Your Live Events by Combining CRM Systems With Marketing Tools

Take advantage of web forms to gather registrations, send out save the date emails and other reminders. You can also connect your CRM system with Eventbrite to collect the most data about the live event you are having.

5. Grow the Power of Your Automated Marketing Tools with CRM Workflows

You can evaluate the answers to your survey and then send any negative responses the department or personal in your company by using the customer workflow in CRM.

6. Use Social Media to Collect Data, Use it And Analyze It

Social media is used to communicate with customers, but why not use your CRM system to collect social networking data and then align it with your other marketing and sales information in a way that will help you to understand your customer much better. Social data offers deep insights that can aid you in your marketing campaigns, as well as, selling to your customers and serving them better.

These are 6 simple things that CRM experts recommend that allow you to get the most out of your marketing through taking advantage of your CRM system to its full capacity.

How to Automate Your CRM Marketing

CRM marketing is a powerful tool that savvy marketers take advantage of. One real advantage is your ability to automate the process. Using the right tools, you can save yourself and staff a great deal of time. Rather than spending your time running campaigns that can be automated you can spend it following your marketing activities and learning what's working and what's not.

Your CRM system offers you the opportunity to instantly access customers and their personal information. With the aid of an eMarketing tool, you can take that information and use it to create marketing campaigns that are scheduled to be sent out at specific times.

Let's have a look at what the workflow would look like.

Step #1 Plan

The first thing you need to do is have a plan. You will determine who your target group is and what content you are going to send them. You will decide on a theme for your campaign or newsletter. For example, you might be sending out a monthly newsletter that's full of helpful tips or you might be putting together a campaign for a promotional item or big sale.

Your themes will change depending on what it is you are trying to accomplish.

Step #2 Production

Here is where you will design the actual mailing using your eMarketing tool. You will add your text and whatever images you want in the mailing. You can create landing pages that when your viewer clicks the link will take them instantly to that landing page. You can include as many links as you want. Even in your newsletter these should be thought of as sales opportunity

Step #3 Follow Up

Ironically, this is where many marketers fall down. They send out their campaigns and that's the end of it. You will want to look at your mailing report so that you can see what's working and what's not. In your mailing report you will be able to see what links your readers are clicking and you will even be able tell what content they prefer. You will get an excellent look at what it is your readers are interested in.

When you use an eMarketing tool that's fully integrated with your CRM you can automate many of the functionality, such as add anyone who clicks on specific link in your mailout and tag them for later action, or you can add people by specific interests. Just as easily, you can remove people.

For a long time CRM has been associated with sales but CRM actually stands for Customer Relationship Management and your marketing is a key part of that. Today is the day to start taking advantage of this powerful tool in your marketing.

CRM Marketing Needs To Align With Multiple Technologies

If you are going to create customer relationship management that is highly effective at the enterprise level you are going to need to create a database strategy that incorporates many different technologies along with integrating different business functionality such as sales, customer service and marketing.

If you really want to get the most out of your CRM technology, marketing needs to have a solid relationship with the IT Dept. This is not the same type of alignment that marketing would have with sales. The IT Dept deals with installing, maintaining, and supporting technology within the organization and they make the decisions about technology. When marketing correctly aligns with the IT Dept, they will be able to get access to the marketing systems they need to achieve their goal and get the marketing outcomes they desire.

It takes time to build this relationship with the IT Dept, so start earlier rather than later. It will be especially beneficial to you. It's also important not to get IT involved too late in your CRM strategies. The earlier you integrate them, the better they will understand your needs and the more help they can be to you.

If you are using cloud based software you will need to have your IT Dept involved because there are many concern for your other data systems. Everything needs to be compatible, privacy needs to be ensured, and it must be secure. You need to your IT Dept's help here!

Another excellent alignment is with sales. Sales already has the data relating to current customers and in that, data will be trends that can help you with your current marketing campaigns. However, in today's world it's also important to reach out beyond the sales department.

For example, savvy CRM marketers are turning to social networking and integrating that into the CRM database. Again, here's a need for your IT Dept. Social media offers you an incredible amount of data on potential customers, such as what they like, what they watch, what they follow, personal information, and the list goes on. This information, when integrated with existing database information can be used to create powerful CRM marketing campaigns that are second to none.

To date, there has never been the ability to easily collect so much information on customers and potential customers. The use of social media is affordable and readily available. Many refer to it as the biggest marketing tool to ever be available.

The key is to make sure you are taking advantage of multiple technologies and venues to gather the information you need to build a strong and effective marketing campaign.

Are You Ready to Use CRM in Your Marketing?

Marketing is key to the success of your company, because without new customers your business will eventually grow stagnant. The exception is if you are constantly offering new products that your existing customers will be interested in. With either scenario, your marketing is important for your success.

You can do everything you need to do manually. People have been marketing manually for decades, but the question is why would you want to when you have a powerful tool like the CRM system. You can be far more effective and it will allow you to grow your business much easier. For many years CRM systems cost so much that small business wasn't interested, but in recent years that's changed significantly, so do yourself a favor and explore whether a CRM system would be beneficial to you.

Let us first look at when you do not need CRM:

CRM means you have to spend money, but the real cost is more than just the fee you pay each month. CRM must be correctly implemented once you have chosen the right solution for your business. It will need to be integrated with your other software. You will also have to hire a specialized staff or contract person to take care of the integration and train people.

You also need your sales and marketing team to be excited and buy into using CRM to make it worthwhile. If your sales team is entering the information consistently and right after any sale, you will have a very strong base for leads and generating marketing campaigns, but if they aren't interested and are not doing it correctly you will have wasted your money.

If your lead flow is low and you have a slow growth trajectory, you might want to use a spreadsheet for now. It isn't fancy but it will do the job until you increase your leads and customer conversions.

Now let's look at when you need to have a CRM system working for you:

If you are growing out of the small business, phase or you are already out of the 'mom and month. CRM must be correctly implemented once you have chosen the right solution for your business. It will need to be integrated with your other software. You will also have to hire a specialized staff or contract person to take care of the integration and train people.

You also need your sales and marketing team to be excited and buy into using CRM to make it worthwhile. If your sales team is entering the information consistently and right after any sale, you will have a very strong base for leads and generating marketing campaigns, but if they aren't interested and are not doing it correctly you will have wasted your money.

If your lead flow is low and you have a slow growth trajectory, you might want to use a spreadsheet for now. It isn't fancy but it will do the job until you increase your leads and customer conversions.

Now let's look at when you need to have a CRM system working for you:

If you are growing out of the small business, phase or you are already out of the 'mom and pop' stage that we talked about earlier, then you need CRM. The earlier you implement it the better. Many successful small companies have significant growth early on with leads growing by leaps and bounds. Then you NEED a CRM system now. Manually trying to track your customers and potential customers will quickly become a nightmare.

Think about it. Tracking 20 or 30 customers or leads in a database is easy. Tracking a 100 becomes very time consuming and over a 100 not only is it slow and a waste of your valuable time (time is money) you will have a cumbersome system that is not very effective. It's time to get your CRM setup and running, otherwise, you'll have a large part of your labor force focusing on maintaining a spreadsheet rather than doing their marketing or selling jobs.

Get your CRM system up and running today and begin to enjoy the many benefits including the ability to create effective marketing campaigns.

Why Do Marketers Use CRM Systems for Their Metrics?

Recent surveys have indicated that today's marketers are turning to CRM systems more than any of the other tools available to them to see their marketing metrics. Realistically, this is a good choice, since the CRM system when used properly can be a key player their marketing campaigns. There are three great reasons why you should be using your CRM system to measure your marketing results. Let's have a look at them.

1. Improves Working with Sales Dept.

When marketing and sales meet to explore the impact of marketing that measures success it will directly impact your revenue. Usually the information you as a marketer need to see is much different from the information the sales department needs to see. Sales people spend most of their time in the CRM software tracking opportunities, measuring their sales and doing forecasts. Marketing results can have this same information made available to them. So rather than your marketing team trying to determine why data is mismatched, both your sales and marketing personal can focus on driving revenue more effectively.

2. Executives Can Compare Results

For the executives the CRM software make many parts of their job much easier. CRM software doesn't just track revenue; it tracks the source of that revenue, which is broken into channels, marketing campaigns or sales. This means marketing can easily see how they compare with other company investments. It's common for marketing campaigns to be strong at bringing in a high volume of potential customers, but often the sell through in the sales department is slower and takes time for those prospects to actually mature and make a purchase. Executives can see these numbers and they can direct according to the company's goals

3. Marketers Can See Sales Relation to Marketing Campaign

The CRM system stores pipeline date, which is core information. Sales staff will often create new opportunities within the CRM system that may have initially came through a marketing campaign thereby starting the beginning of the sales cycle. When the data is tied together marketing team through contact information and campaign responses then the marketing team is able to the influence of a campaign to a sales opportunity with accuracy. This is important to knowing whether a campaign is effective and providing a good ROI.

Taking full advantage of your CRM software for marketing is a great way to increase your customers, your ROI and ultimately your revenue.

Traditional CRM Software vs. Marketing Automation Software

There seems to be a lot of buzz around CRM software and marketing automation. If you aren't really sure what the difference is, or why you are being told to use your CRM software as part of your marketing strategy, you'll want to read on.

Traditional CRM software focuses on sales, while marketing automation software focuses on marketing. Okay, you probably already figured that much out. So let's delve in a little further. CRM traditionally tracks customer information such as name, address, email, phone number and purchases along with complaints or calls for customer service.

On the flip side, marketing automation software streamlines and automates the marketing process and then provides tools to measure the success. Marketing software stores similar information such as names, address, email, phone number, etc. Marketing software lets you follow a prospect's activities at the top of the funnel. For example, when they opened an email, visited a website, stopped by a social media site. Marketing software also lets you schedule your marketing campaigns.

The goal of marketing automation is to foster leads and prepare them for the sales team once the lead reaches the bottom of the funnel. This is where most companies begin to track the interaction with the prospect who is now a customer, using CRM software. Now when the sales team speaks with a customer they see a full picture of whom that customer is thanks to the profile that's been built.

CRM software can become part of your marketing strategy. Most CRM packages will integrate with marketing automation software. Of course, you will need to do your homework to find the best blend for you. Newer CRM programs are also being released with a marketing component built right into them, which is the perfect scenario.

By integrating your marketing with your CRM, it provides some powerful information. Now the sales staff knows a lot about this prospect before they ever have made their purchase, which sets them up to better do their job. In addition, integration allows the tracking of the entire time in the pipeline. Depending on the product(s) being sold this can be a slow process. Knowing all of this helps to better determine the success of a particular marketing campaign and whether changes need to be made. You can also easily determine your ROI, which is important.

In today's hi-tech world, your CRM and marketing software should be fully integrated if you want to really have a streamlined approach to sales.

Social Media Changes CRM

For tech watchers, this is pretty big news. CRM Software supports are quickly acquiring startups that allow businesses to comfortably manage significantly more social media platforms, as well as, a variety of platforms.

Oracle has purchased Vitrue to aid in the managing and publishing of social media campaigns. They've also purchased Collective Intellect to aid in the monitoring of social chatter. Salesforce.com, a strong CRM contender purchased Radian6 a sentiment tracking company. The list goes on. The question is why the big shopping spree and why should you care?

It seems industry experts believe that the next five years are going to be key for chief marketing officers, who will spend a huge amount of money on CRM systems that will integrate social media. This is great news for any business that isn't running around with a seven-figure technology budget. Early game players referred to as Social CRM adopters are setting the stage for much smaller companies who have limited budgets to be able to adopt these new method fast and within their budget. In addition, it will be without the problems that have troubled CRM programs in the past.

Traditional CRM is integrated to make life more efficient and faster customer service within an organization and its departments. It's designed to increase profits, improve customer service with faster resolutions and many other benefits.

However, when CRM programs are not executed properly they can actually they can actually make a company look very bad. Anyone who has received a mailout that's supposed to look personalized but the name is spelled incorrectly or duplicates are received, knows that a company's customer service attempts are far from personal. Another great example is the automated telephone answering system that annoys customers to no end. Yes all of these things lower your costs but at what cost to your customer service end?

Traditional CRM systems turn people into data and that's a problem. Relationships become rules of engagement and that's an even bigger problem. Technology can't be budget. In addition, it will be without the problems that have troubled CRM programs in the past.

Traditional CRM is integrated to make life more efficient and faster customer service within an organization and its departments. It's designed to increase profits, improve customer service with faster resolutions and many other benefits.

However, when CRM programs are not executed properly they can actually they can actually make a company look very bad. Anyone who has received a mailout that's supposed to look personalized but the name is spelled incorrectly or duplicates are received, knows that a company's customer service attempts are far from personal. Another great example is the automated telephone answering system that annoys customers to no end. Yes all of these things lower your costs but at what cost to your customer service end?

Traditional CRM systems turn people into data and that's a problem. Relationships become rules of engagement and that's an even bigger problem. Technology can't be empathetic, which is what's driving CRM companies to integrate with social media.

75% of American consumers use one or more social networking sites, which provides the opportunity for 24/7 exceptional customer service, smart branding, and endless opportunities to manipulate the consumer in your favor. A company's data power increases exponentially. It's adding an entirely new dimension to CRM and that's exciting.

For years, CRM has been one-sided communication and now that social media is becoming an integrated part of CRM the opportunity for two-sided communication is a reality. Its smart business and those who jump in early will really benefit.

Take Advantage of CRM Marketing

For many small businesses, it can be difficult to develop a solid marketing campaign. First, it is cost prohibitive. It is also difficult to manage. As a result, small businesses tend to ignore strong marketing, which ultimately results in a loss of profits and revenue. CRM marketing automation solutions can change that, because now you can have precision marketing and get results, on a budget that you can afford.

CRM marketing allows you to develop marketing campaigns that target a specific group based on your customer history. You can quickly and easily send out email campaigns on promotions that are time sensitive or you can send out newsletters. You can also track your marketing expenses in real time. CRM marketing lets you focus on the quality of the leads you generate so that you increase your ROI.

Using CRM marketing you can target your market activities and define what your success metrics will look like for each campaign. Marketers know how important ROI is, but without accurate data, it's next to impossible to accurately calculate your ROI. Now you'll know and you'll be able to adjust accordingly.

Because of the improved email marketing, you will have the opportunity to create dynamic templates that are interesting and effective. You can easily scrub your mailing list so that it is always accurate. Setup emails that comply with the CAN-SPAM act and schedule mass email campaigns to go on a desire schedule. It's that simple. You'll never again struggle to reach your customers.

In addition, CRM marketing lets you track the performance of your campaign(s) so you can easily make changes. You can track on a number of parameters, which give you the flexibility to see what you need to see. You can access this information online or create reports for upper management. You can also present that information in your report in a dynamic fashion so that management can quickly grasp your successes. This makes it much easier to ask for a bigger marketing budget, when they can clearly see that the ROI is good.

CRM marketing is a powerful tool that is often overlooked or underutilized. The information that is available to you in your CRM database creates a powerful profile of who your customer is and it makes it easier to target new customers along with your existing customers. This is especially true if you take advantage of social networking and begin to incorporate that information into your CRM marketing. Don't miss out on a powerful way to increase the effectiveness of your marketing.

How to Automate Your Marketing Campaigns Using CRM

One of the most underused tools in marketing is the CRM system. Many companies are running anywhere from a handful to thousands of campaigns at one time and each must be managed. There can be campaigns to sell a new product, there can be campaigns for new customers, there can be cross selling, and the list goes on. Trying to manage multiple campaigns that are all different can be time consuming, even when it's just a handful. The error rate is also high and sometimes it's virtually impossible to manage.

What makes things even trickier is that successful campaigns need you to be able to have access to all of the information at one time, not have to pick and choose from various places. These campaigns can become very complex and so the best way to take care of them is simply to take advantage of your CRM system.

A CRM system that is well run can help you run smoothly, improve your marketing campaign response rate, remove most of the challenges, and improve your ROI.

Target Market

You will be able to target your market with ease. Select candidates based on purchases, demographics, responses to a survey or any other way you want. Choose one or more criteria to include to pull your marketing campaign recipients right out of your database. Targeted marketing is always far more effective at bringing people into the pipeline than just random marketing.

Manage Execution

Even the best campaign will not do well if you cannot systematically execute it. CRM can help you to track your campaigns on a real time basis so you know exactly what is going on at any time. It can help you to maintain a schedule for your marketing campaigns and you can even set them to automatically launch. Using the CRM system provides you with all the necessary flexibility to be successful with your campaign.

Follow Up in a Timely Manner

This is a very important step and yet marketers often fail here. An automated marketing system can follow up for you at the preset date and time ensuring your potential customers receive the second part of your marketing campaign.

With CRM, you have the ability to track the status of every single lead. You know whether you contacted them in a timely way, what the outcome was, where they are in the pipeline, whether they actually made a purchase. The information is all there. Having the ability to see the effectiveness of your campaign through the entire sales cycle is a powerful tool that far too many are overlooking.

Let Your Inbound Marketing Plan Define the CRM You Choose

CRM products aren't new; they've actually been around longer than the web was used as a business tool. The first CRM software was called ACT and it dates to 1987. Fast forward to now. CRM products have many additional features have been added including a number of features borrowed from automated marketing products. Some of these technologies overlap, while others compete. Senior management is constantly bulking at the idea of having to buy both CRM software and marketing software, so rather than asking for both why not let your inbound marketing plan define what you look for in a CRM option.

Inbound marketing is all about the use of search technologies combined with content marketing to nurture the best prospects and attract them to what you have to offer. For some companies this is a complete change in their selling approach.

The time has come to reinvent your sales process. Finally, your sales process can be prospects that are broke down based on their areas of interest and other information they volunteer. As you nurture this relationship, their content path will constantly provide you with more information discretely and on a real time basis. You can now spend less time prospecting and more time closing sales.

As you rebuild the way, you take care of sales you may discover that Lead Relationship management can be much more valuable in achieving your goals than Customer Relationship management, so when you go to buy CRM software you should choose a system that emphasizes this. Because rather than focusing on tracking purchases and the communication that follows after, you want to be able to focus on their interaction on your social media sites and websites and the situational and attitudinal information that they provide in exchange for the relevant content you provide.

Once you know what direction you are headed you can find CRM software that will play nice with your marketing automation needs and the need for multiple software packages can go by the wayside. You might be surprised to learn that you will not have to spend a fortune to get marketing functionality. Of course, it will depend on exactly what you need. There are a number of providers so make sure you do your homework in-depth.

By knowing what it is you need and how you visualize it integrating with the sales database, you'll not only choose the best CRM software, you'll simplify the process and make access to data from leads and customers readily available.

Incorporate Current Marketing Channels With CRM

CRM software plays an important role in many companies, but a major advantage in your marketing awaits you, when you use a completely integrated approach with your CRM that includes making use of the various technology components to track, improve your customer data and your customer service.

Social media platforms should play a key role in your CRM marketing strategies as they offer a completely new source for customer data, and marketers should be adding them to their CRM databases.

Not only has social media given companies access to a multitude of levels of information about potential customers, it also offers a new way to reach your customers that is acceptable and encouraged by social media users. What many companies don't realize is that it will also have a significant impact on the way that B2B companies reach the market.

Having the ability to track behavior, such as what users click on, the websites they visit, what they like, etc., allows marketers to create a 'digital' profile and adding social media to your database will give you insight that you have never had in the past. You will quickly learn what the consumer likes, what they trust, and what they focus on.

As a marketer, it is imperative that you focus on incorporating those results into your database so that you can form a 'big picture' of the consumer and your customers that will allow you to easily target the perspective customers.

Most companies are already using social media themselves. Depending on the size of the account will depend on how many social networks they participate in, but it's common for a large company to manage more than 100 different social media accounts.

B2B companies struggle more with social media. They must merge social interaction with their fundamental practices, which can be challenging. They must also measure social media to learn the channel value. There are customers who might complain on social networking platforms, yet never lodge an actual customer service ticket. This technology allows you to grab that customers name and actually deal with the complaint that otherwise you would not have known about. It builds good customer service and good branding.

All of the information gathered in social networks helps to build a better picture of your buyer. This information is helpful throughout the selling cycle where marketing is targeting potential buyers of your product. There is great potential here when used properly.

CRM and Email Marketing

Email marketing is one of the most powerful types of marketing you have available to you, so it's important to get it right. If you currently

www.ingramcontent.com/pod-product-compliance
Lightning Source LLC
Chambersburg PA
CBHW071239220526
45468CB00002B/922